MW01593694

"MY NAME IS (STATE YOUR NAME), AND I AM A WRITER"

C. G. COOPER

TABLE OF CONTENTS

CHAPTER 1
LOST AND LONELY

S herri sighed as she pushed open the heavy wooden door that led to the inner sanctum of her favorite coffee shop. Faded concert posters and the smell of roasted cinnamon greeted her entrance.

She'd been coming for years, enticed by ever-present aroma of artisan coffee and just baked pastries. It was her place to get away, a place where she felt at home and comfortable. Most importantly, she was surrounded by the artsy middle class that seemed to blanket the establishment on a twenty-four hours a day.

They were what she wanted to be, a person passionate about her profession.

She would often sit beside a tight-knit group of conspirators, she, pretending to be reading some thoughtful piece on her shiny laptop, they, talking animatedly about their latest piece of writing, cool new tech start-up or mission trip to Guatemala.

She envied them and often dreamed of being one of them.

But that was impossible. Sherri had a full-time job in a one of the largest high-rise office buildings in the city. Her mother said she was lucky to have a good job. A lot of people didn't She'd bounced around from employer to employer after college trying to find the 'right fit'. She landed in the office building four blocks from the coffee shop.

On the weekends Sherri immersed herself in movies, concerts, off Broadway plays and the local community. She'd once thought that a career as a screenwriter or maybe even a freelance writer were possible. But so many people, mostly friends and family, had told her that being any kind of artist, let alone a writer, was an impossible dream.

The advice had stuck and she'd withdrawn from a creative writing course in her first year at college. She still had the one and only story she'd written tucked away in her grandmother's old jewelry box.

Some nights Sherri would grab a glass of oaky chardonnay and read the short story. It wasn't bad but it certainly wasn't good. Still, she loved that she had written it.

She sauntered up to the counter and ordered her usual. The bored dreadlocked employee nodded with a smile and wordlessly swiped Sherri's card and handed her a receipt.

Her latte piping hot and ready, Sherri grabbed a handful of napkins (she was always careful around her prized 'writing' laptop) and headed toward a secluded booth in back of the shop.

Today she was all business. She had a mission, a goal.

I will finish my first chapter, she thought to herself for perhaps the fiftieth time that morning. It was Saturday. She had all day. *Easy peasy.*

Two hours, three lattes, one banana nut muffin and two chocolate croissants later, Sherri sat staring at the blinking cursor on her screen.

What is wrong with me? she thought.

The only thing on the crystal clear screen, other than the dot-dot-dotting cursor, were the words *Chapter One*.

She adjusted her noise-cancelling headphones that were trying to urge her inner muse with Enya-like tranquility. It wasn't working.

Putting her face in her hands, Sherri didn't notice that her perfectly sharpened and ready for duty pencil had rolled off the Formica table and onto the wooden floor.

A second later she felt a tap on her shoulder and almost jumped. Whipping around in near panic, her elbow managed to sweep the corner of her prized laptop and she watched helplessly as it slid off the edge of the table. Reaching a desperate hand out to catch it, she grasped a handful of air as another hand gracefully snagged the computer and set it quietly back in its place.

Sherri turned slowly and looked up at her savior. As she opened her mouth to thank the person a million times for saving the laptop she really couldn't afford, her voice caught. Standing above her with a crooked grin was a man she instantly recognized.

He was a fixture at the coffee shop. When he wasn't clacking away on his laptop, the popular young man with a head full of unkempt hair was chatting away happily with other patrons.

The man's mouth was moving, but Sherri couldn't hear any words. It took her a second to realize that she still had her headphones on. Turning scarlet, she carefully removed the Zen inducers and laid them on the table.

"Everything okay?" the man asked again.

"Umm, yes. Thanks for catching my laptop."

"No problem." Still grinning, the man peeked over Sherri's shoulder. "What are you working on?"

There wasn't any accusation in his voice, in fact, he seemed genuinely interested, but Sherri still snapped the laptop shut like she was protecting a CIA secret.

"Oh nothing," she answered, trying to sound nonchalant. "Just a little writing."

The man's eyebrows rose.

"Really? What are you writing about?"

"I uh…"

"I only ask because I'm a writer too. Always love to hear what other people are working on. Inspiration, you know?"

"Well, it's about…well you see…I'm not really a…" Sherri huffed and her chin dropped to her chest. Suddenly all the frustration of the last two hours came flooding out like an uncontrollable fire hose. "I've really been sitting here for the last two hours trying to come up with something, but I can't…I can't…"

The man nodded with a knowing look. "Mind if I sit down?"

Sherri nodded sadly and motioned to the other chair. Before sitting down, the man unslung his battered leather messenger bag and offered his hand.

"I'm Daniel."

CHAPTER 2

MY NAME IS...

Daniel slumped down easily and stared at Sherri for a moment. A mischievous smile crept onto his face.

"What?" asked Sherri.

"Aren't you going to tell me your name?"

"Right. Sorry. I'm Sherri."

"Nice to meet you, Sherri."

"Nice to meet you too, Daniel."

"So, what seems to be the problem? Writer's block?"

Sherri didn't know how to respond. It wasn't that she was necessarily attracted to the man, but he had a calm composure that unsettled her. She considered asking him politely to mind his own business. Then again, what could it hurt?

"I wish it was writer's block. More like writer's Great Wall of China," she sighed.

Daniel chuckled and shifted in his chair. He waved to another person Sherri didn't know, then turned his attention squarely back to her.

"I know the feeling. How long have you been a writer?"

"I'm, uh, not really a writer."

Daniel nodded with slightly pursed lips and scratched his stubbly chin.

"So why are you here?"

Why did I open my big mouth? She felt trapped and embarrassed. Finally, she closed her eyes and said, "I don't know about being a writer, but I just, I feel happy every time I sit in this place."

Daniel smiled and grabbed his well-worn bag. Sherri was sure she'd scared him off and that he was about to walk away and find some 'real' writers to talk to. Instead, after a second of rooting around, Daniel pulled out a small blue pad of sticky notes and a pen. Covering what he was doing with his non-writing hand so she couldn't see, he wrote something and then flipped the pad over.

"Okay. If I'm going to help you, you need to read what's on this sticky note."

Sherri's eyes went wide. "But, I didn't ask for…"

"I know, I know. You didn't ask for my help. But it couldn't hurt?"

Sherri stared at Daniel's hands dreading whatever was on that small piece of blue paper.

"Why would you want to help me?" she asked, her voice barely above a whisper.

"Let's just say that I've had more than my fair share of help along the way. Pay it forward, right?"

Sherri found herself bobbing her head as a glimmer of hope shone through the fog of misery.

"Great. Now, you promise to read this out loud?" Daniel asked, suddenly serious. "This might be the most important thing I help you do."

Sherri nodded.

Daniel slid the overturned pad across the table. Sherri flipped it over slowly scared of what she might find.

In neat lettering Daniel had written:

My Name is (state your name), and I am a Writer.

Sherri reread the note to herself and looked up, not understanding. "You want me to read this?"

"Yeah. I mean, don't say the part in parenthesis, say your name instead, but say the whole thing."

What is this guy talking about? Sherri thought. Was he teasing her? She'd never liked the idea of speaking in public. Just the thought of reading the short note made her stomach turn. Summoning some hidden well of courage, Sherri took a hitched breath and read.

"My name is Sherri, and I am a writer."

"Well done. Now, as one writer to another, are you ready?"

"Ready for what? I...I don't know what you're talking about."

Daniel leaned back and folded his hands across his stomach. "Sherri, what do you think is the qualification for being a writer?"

"I don't know. I guess you have to go to school, take courses. Stuff like that."

"What if I told you that none of that matters?" asked Daniel.

Sherri's insecurity was telling her that she was being toyed with. And yet, Daniel didn't seem to be joking. From her long hours of babysitting company clients, Sherri had a pretty good internal BS detector. After a moment, she decided to play along.

"Okay. Why doesn't it matter?"

Daniel's eyebrow arched as if to say he could sense her disbelief.

"Let me come at it a different way. You have to go to medical school to be a doctor, right?"

"Yes."

"And all pilots have to got to flight school?"

"Uh huh."

"Is there a similar school for writers?"

Sherri thought about the question. She'd never heard of a specific 'writing' school.

"I guess you could major in English or something."

"Fair enough. I mentioned earlier that I am a writer. How many books do you think I've written?"

Sherri didn't have a clue and almost told him as much. "I don't know. Two?"

Daniel smiled warmly, and without a hint of conceit replied, "Actually, I've published eleven."

"Really?" Sherri blurted.

"Yes. And do you know what I majored in?"

"English?" she asked, almost sheepishly.

Daniel shook his head. "I never finished college. Spent a year there, but it didn't take. I wasn't mature enough at the time."

"So you're some kind of savant or something?"

Daniel ignored the question. "How long do you think it took me to write those eleven books?"

Sherri knew she wasn't going to believe the answer, but replied anyway.

"Fifteen years?"

"Actually I only started writing a little over two years ago."

Sherri's mouth dropped open. Daniel laughed.

"I promise I'm not lying to you. Here, look," Daniel pulled out his smart phone and loaded a webpage. He scrolled through his list of books.

"But, how?"

Daniel shrugged. "Two and half years ago I was in the same boat as you. I wanted to write something, except I had a laundry list of insecurities and made up rules holding me back. Let's go back to what we were talking about before. Who told you that you had to get an English degree to become a writer?"

"I don't know. I guess I just…assumed."

"Assumption's a dangerous thing. We *assume* we can't do something because of a conversation we've heard or some story a friend told us. Here's the point. Anyone can be a writer. As long as you can string a few words together and sound halfway coherent, you can be a writer. Now that's not to say that everyone will make it, we do have to hone our craft, but nowadays there is zero barrier to entry. Anyone can be a writer."

Daniel let the thought sink in. Sherri face stayed scrunched in confusion. Daniel's words went against everything she'd ever thought or heard. Could it be possible that anyone could, if they put their mind to it, be a writer?

Her faced calmed and she looked up slowly, awe in her eyes as if she'd just woken up from a strange yet wonderful dream.

"Does that mean I can be a writer?" she asked.

"Of course. Why don't you read that sticky note again."

Sherri looked down at the blue pad and read, "My Name is Sherri, and I am a Writer." She looked back up, a smile stretching from ear to ear.

PRACTICE

It's your turn. Go some place private and read the following line adding your name to the middle:

My Name is (*state your name*), and I am a Writer.

That wasn't so hard, was it? Now take out a piece of paper and write it down with your name included. Post it somewhere that you will see it throughout the day. The perfect place might be your computer, bathroom, kitchen, wallet, cubicle, etc… It doesn't matter where, just pick a place that's visible to you.

Repeat this line over and over throughout the day, day after day. Send your proclamation out into the world. The first step is belief that you are a writer.

NOTES

NOTES

CHAPTER 3
FINDING YOUR VOICE

S herri left their first impromptu meeting giddy with excitement. Every day she looked at her new mantra

My Name is Sherri, and I am a Writer

Every day she repeated it during breaks from clients, on the way to the fridge, during lunch, in the shower, walking her dog… It got to the point that Sherri started to believe what she was saying.

You see, the power of thought and projection were helping Sherri make the mental shift. The initial seeds of hope were growing into a need to do more.

They'd agreed to meet the following Saturday at 9am. Daniel had instructed her to only bring some paper, a pen and an open mind. As Saturday crept closer, and Sherri's excitement grew, she could only wonder what the next lesson would be.

She'd already devoured two of Daniel's books and was halfway into the third. Savoring the easy flow and simple storytelling, Sherri hoped she could one day attain the same level of written finesse.

Saturday finally rolled around and Sherri half sprinted to the coffee shop. Her pulse quickened as she neared. Taking a steadying breath, she opened the door and stepped into her tiny haven.

Inside the tables were packed. It took her a minute to find Daniel in the crowd. He was sitting in a corner booth across from an older gentleman in a tweed jacket and horn-rimmed glasses.

Sherri's stomach dropped as she quickly looked at her phone to confirm that she was on time. Avoiding eye contact, she made her way over to Daniel's table. Before she could apologize for some made up triviality, Daniel rose and greeted her. The older man followed suit.

"Sherri, this is my good friend Professor Jenkins."

Sherri nervously shook hands with the grey haired academic.

"It's a pleasure to meet you, Sherri. Daniel tells me you're a writer as well."

Sherri blushed and averted her eyes.

"Don't worry," Prof. Jenkins offered, "I felt the same way not so long ago."

Daniel waved them into their seats as Sherri dutifully extracted her journal and pen from her oversized purse.

"How was your week?" Daniel asked. "Was our little exercise helpful?"

Sherri smiled shyly. "I think so. I caught myself almost saying it to a couple of clients and I know I had dreams about it."

"That's good. It means the idea is sinking in. Now, are you ready to find your voice?"

"I'm not sure I know what you mean," said Sherri, writing *Find My Voice* on the first page of her journal.

"We each have a different style of writing. Some people call it our Voice. It's how we come across and it's not unlike our personality. For example, you might work with a busy body that talks and talks all day. Can't get a word in. Their written voice may or may not be similar. I asked Professor Jenkins to stop by so he could tell you his story. Professor?"

Prof. Jenkins cleared his throat and chuckled deeply. It was a pleasant sound that reminded Sherri of her great uncle who smelled like pipe tobacco and vanilla.

"I've been a philosophy and literature teacher for close to thirty years. Naturally I've read most of the works of Aristotle, Socrates, Yates, to name a few.

You might call my background rather highbrow. Over the years, I've written certain position papers and theses to compliment my teaching and advance my tenure. Ten years ago I made the fateful decision to write my first book. From the start, things didn't go well. I struggled to get more than a few paragraphs in before quitting in disgust. The same scene played out repeatedly until about a year ago. By then, I had what I thought was a very satisfactory tome of new age philosophy."

"What happened a year ago?" Sherri asked.

Prof. Jenkins sipped his tea and smiled. "I met our friend Daniel here."

Daniel interrupted. "I was typing away one beautiful Sunday when I looked up to see the Professor chatting with some colleagues in this very booth. The others looked very excited and were obviously gushing over him."

"Daniel's right. I'd just published my work through an academic publisher. My colleagues were thrilled…but I wasn't."

"Why not?" asked Sherri.

"Daniel, why don't you tell her what happened next."

Daniel nodded. "After peeking over a couple of times, just being curious, I got the feeling that the

Professor was, how would I put it...not really joining in on the celebration. It seemed that he was more than just exceedingly humble. He really didn't look like he was enjoying himself. So, me being the way I am," Daniel and Prof. Jenkins chuckled, "I waited until the others had left, and walked over."

"I believe you offered your congratulations to my success," said Jenkins.

"Yeah. It looked like he was trying his darndest to keep a smile on his face. One thing led to another and we ended up talking for two hours." Daniel motioned for Jenkins to finish.

"That's right. Daniel asked me some questions that I found very uncomfortable at the time. Why was I writing? Who was my audience? Did I enjoy the writing process? They were all questions that should've been easy to answer. Instead, I think I mumbled a couple lame responses. Daniel quickly saw through the charade. He knew I wasn't happy."

"Listen to the next part, Sherri. This is where it gets good." Daniel smiled like a ten year old boy who'd just found a treasure map.

"Daniel's questions made me think very hard about why I'd spent the preceding ten years writing a book that I was only marginally proud of. You know what I figured out?"

Sherri shook her head, eager for the punchline.

"I grew up reading almost any paperback I could get my hands on. From Hardy Boys to Louis L'Amour. I loved a great story and still do. There were some weekends that I would read four books, and that was after doing my homework. I still churn through thrillers like I'm in grade school. What Daniel helped me realize was that although philosophy and classical literature were my job, dime store paperbacks, pulp fiction and pop culture thrillers were my passion."

"So why didn't you write in those genres?" asked Sherri.

"I didn't think that was supposed to be my Voice. Remember, I am a member of an elite group of academics. We are supposed to be immersed in our field. During the day I would be, but at night I walked the aisles of bookstores and libraries looking for a Vince Flynn novel or a Tom Clancy thriller I hadn't read yet.

"Daniel helped me discover my true passion and then my voice. At first I tried to write a thriller like a professor. That didn't work. Daniel tasked me with finding my voice. After some fits and starts, I did. I haven't looked back since."

"But...how did you do it?"

Prof. Jenkins smiled warmly. "If I'm not mistaken, that's the next bit of homework Daniel has for you."

Sherri looked at Daniel expectantly, pleading with her eyes.

"Here's what you need to do. Go through your list of favorite authors. Pick three books that you can't put down. You might've read them numerous times. But here's the catch. They have to be in a voice you would use."

"What does that mean?"

"Here's an example, I love Pride and Prejudice. I've read it ten times or more. I enjoy the way Austen ebbs and flows the dialogue and description. Here's the rub. I don't talk that way, and I sure as heck can't write that way. It's not my style. It's not my voice."

"So you're saying find a style that I think I could write in?" asked Sherri.

"Right," answered Daniel. "I don't want you to copy someone, just get inspiration. Your voice will evolve over time. As you perfect your craft you will get better and better. Here's the second piece of your homework: write five hundred words in your Voice. Make up a story. It should feel natural and conversational. Don't try to sound like someone else. Be yourself."

Sherri didn't look completely convinced but said, "Okay. I'll do it."

PRACTICE

It's time to find your voice. Go through the list of books you love. Pick three that you think have a similar style to what your writing approach will be. It can be fiction or non-fiction. Read a few pages out loud. Does it feel natural?

Next, come up with a simple concept. It could be a boy meeting a girl for the first time or a post-apocalyptic zombie invasion. It might be a lesson on how to can pickled yams. Choose something that genuinely interests you. Now write 500 words in your own unique Voice.

When you're finished, read it out loud and see how it feels.

NOTES

NOTES

CHAPTER 4
JOIN THE COMMUNITY

The following Saturday Sherri bounced in brimming with excitement. Daniel was seated alone and caught her eye. He beamed and she had to exert all her self-control to keep from skipping across the café.

"How did it go?" Daniel asked.

The words came out of Sherri like raging waters through a broken dam.

"It was amazing, like a light switch went off in my head. Writing five hundreds words was so easy."

"Can I see?"

Sherri handed him the single sheet of paper. Daniel read it quickly and smiled. "I like it. It sounds like you."

Sherri almost burst into tears with gratitude. Truth be told, she'd been a nervous wreck imagining what Daniel would think of her writing. She'd already read all of his books and hoped to one day be as confident as her new mentor.

"What's next? Another writing assignment?" asked Sherri, eager to feed her budding writer's appetite.

"Not exactly. Grab your stuff. I want to introduce you to some people."

Sherri gathered her things and following Daniel to the largest booth in the place. Three men and a woman were arrayed on either side. These people weren't necessarily strangers to Sherri. She'd seen them all before, but she'd never met them.

They all looked up at the sound of Daniel's approach, smiling in unison.

"Hey, guys!" said Daniel.

Sherri hesitated momentarily until Daniel nudged her forward.

"Sherri, I want you to meet some other awesome writers. Quick loop around the table, Josiah, Patrice, Frank and Amber. Everyone, this is Sherri."

They all shook hands and scooted over to make room for her and Daniel. Sherri stared in wonder. These were the people she'd always wanted to be with. Now that she really took the time to look, they were all very unique. Josiah was tall with long sandy hair tied in a ponytail. Patrice was a short man with a dark complexion whose accent reminded Sherri of her one and only trip to France. Frank's brilliant white smile contrasted with the obsidian skin that bulged beneath his Under Armor shirt. Amber sat demurely, hands folded neatly in her lap, her short brown hair partially hiding her face.

"I wanted you to meet our little crew. Everyone's a writer of some sort. Frank is a songwriter, Patrice writes biographies, Josiah write tutorials, and Amber write novels."

"You've gotta check out Amber's stuff, Sherri," boomed Frank. "She makes more money than all the rest of us, well, except for maybe Daniel. Her stuff is on point."

Amber nodded politely and smiled. Sherri just stared. If asked, Amber would've been the last person she would've chosen to be the most successful. It was obvious in the way the others admired her that Amber was something special.

Daniel rapped his knuckles on the table. "Order in the court."

Everyone chuckled and turned their attention back to the affable leader.

"Like I was saying, I wanted to introduce you to these guys so you can start building your community. Another huge part of being a writer is reaching out and meeting your peers. I won't go into the details, but I went through a really lonely stretch where it was just me and my writing. I felt like a cave troll. I finally crawled out into the light and stumbled into this place. After making myself meet other artists, my attitude and my writing improved."

Heads were nodding all around the table. Surprisingly, it was Amber who spoke first.

"You might not get this vibe from me, but I've been pretty shy since I was a kid."

"It's what makes her write awesome slasher thrillers!" laughed Frank.

Amber giggled. "He's probably right. All that time alone gave me a lot of time to think. The problem was that I had all these ideas and no one to share them with."

Sherri's brow scrunched. "How exactly did other writers help you?"

"Not in the way you might think. Most writers are pretty selfish without even knowing it. They get into writing groups to get feedback on their work then leave."

"Isn't that what you're supposed to do?" asked Sherri, visibly confused.

"Sure. That's part of it. But what we've all learned with Daniel's help is that it's better to give first."

"Give? Give what?" Sherri blurted. The last thing she needed was to shell out money for help. The laptop splurge had necessitated an emergency spending freeze and a tighter than normal budget. She had nothing to give.

Amber smiled warmly. "We give by being here for each other. Sometimes it's to give feedback on a manuscript, other times it's to give pointers on marketing or even personal stuff. Trust me, when I learned that I would get far more in return just by giving to my friends, I was all in."

"Amber's right. There's this weird thing that happens when we help others. It's like the universe is giving us something too," Daniel said.

"I'm still not clear on what you mean by getting something back," said Sherri.

"Let me give you an example," started Daniel. "Let's say Amber is working on the launch of her new book. She comes to us asking for our thoughts. By going through the process we not only help her, we're also perfecting the system in our heads. That way, when it comes time for us to do something similar, the case study has already been done. I can't tell you how many times that's happened to me."

"It's all about stories," said Josiah. "Daniel is a story collector. It's why we all gravitate toward him.

He listens without an ulterior motive. By helping others in an unselfish way he's also helped himself."

Daniel waved away the compliment. "Thanks for going deep on us, Josiah," he smirked with a playful roll of his eyes. "But he's right. Almost the second that I started helping others, my writing improved. I had more ideas. I woke up refreshed. There wasn't an obstacle I couldn't overcome."

"So you're saying I can...hang out with you guys?" Sherri asked quietly.

"Of course, girl!" said Frank, throwing his hands in the air. "The more the merrier!"

They all laughed and Sherri was too relieved to know what to say. She settled in as Patrice let them in on the latest dilemma he needed help with.

PRACTICE

Remember the phrase, "I shall give before I receive." It may sound corny or spiritual, but believe it.

Now look around and find a small group of writers. Ask your friends if they know of any open writing groups.

Starting online may be easier if you're a little squeamish about going face-to-face from the start. An excellent resource are Groups on LinkedIn. Other writers post questions that they'd love answered. It's an easy place to start.

You can also go on sites like TheWritePractice.com. Make it a habit to give other writers feedback on their work.

The goal is to offer your assistance to others. Get a feel for the group. Open up. Do some light proofreading or give your two cents on a blog post.

Your mission is to engage with the writing community. Get used to reaching out and helping others.

NOTES

NOTES

CHAPTER 5
WRITE, WRITE, WRITE

O ver the next week Sherri met with the coffeehouse crew (that's what Frank called it) three more times. Sometimes they were missing a member, but for Sherri it didn't matter. She was an eager helper and offered to read excerpts, brainstorm ideas or just listen. The process showed Sherri that her opinion was valued and that it was inevitable that she'd learn something that would aid her own writing.

By the time her Saturday meet-up with Daniel rolled around, Sherri had joined three groups on LinkedIn and was actively posting questions and comments. The interaction made her feel alive and, once again, she was hopping with excitement when she entered the coffee shop.

Daniel looked to be deep in writing mode, with eyes narrowed in concentration, so Sherri took her time ordering a latte and a banana nut muffin. By the time she sat down across from Daniel, he'd completed whatever had so fixated his attention.

"Hey, Sherri!"

"Good morning, Daniel. Whatcha working on?"

Daniel shook his head and exhaled in frustration. "A new project. I'm dabbling in a new genre. Still working out the kinks."

"Can I take a peek?" asked Sherri, playfully.

"Not yet. It's still kind of a mess. I'll let you know when it's ready for outside eyes."

Sherri doubted that the manuscript could be as bad as Daniel made it sound, but she didn't push the subject.

"How are things going with your last assignment?" Daniel asked.

Sherri told him.

"That's great. Feels pretty good, huh?"

"I'm really having a hard time focusing on my real job. Every time I get a break I'm checking my email to see if anyone's posted a new comment on LinkedIn. I can't remember the last time I was this excited about something."

Daniel's eyes lit up at Sherri's enthusiasm.

"Are you ready for your next mission?"

Sherri nodded eagerly. She hadn't touched her coffee or muffin.

"Okay. This one's really simple. It's also the hardest."

"What do you mean?"

Daniel scratched his stubbly chin. "What's a writer's job?"

"To write?"

"Exactly! So why is it that so many writers waste time doing anything but?"

Sherri stared at Daniel willing the answer to come.

"Because we're human?"

"Bingo! We let anything and everything get in the way of what we're really supposed to be doing, which is writing. Are you ready for the secret antidote?"

Sherri had a feeling she knew where Daniel was going and nodded with a warm smile.

"Write every day. It doesn't matter if you write a paragraph, ten thousand words, a sonnet. Write every single day. Sometimes I sit under a tree and write a song. It's all about creating the habit. What do the experts say? Do something for twenty-seven days and it becomes a habit? Well they're right. It should feel like a compulsion or an addiction. When a day goes by that you don't write it should feel like an itch that you just can't scratch. That's your subconscious telling you that it's time to write.

"Your homework for the coming week is to write something every single day. Remember, it doesn't matter how long it is, although I would prefer you write at least five hundred words."

Sherri nodded and took a sip of her latte.

PRACTICE

For the next seven days, write something every day. Just like Daniel told Sherri, it doesn't matter what you write. It can be a story about your childhood, a poem about the ocean, a comedic blurb about your boss, your favorite recipe…

Don't stop at seven days. If you're serious about writing you should do it every day. Don't let the lack of a computer stop you. Jot something down on a pad of paper or an old napkin. Just write.

Need more ideas? Here are more writing prompts:

- Pick one word from the dictionary and write about it for ten minutes.
- Describe, in detail, the best thing you've ever eaten.
- Describe, in detail, the time you were most scared.
- Write a poem about pink horses and yellow lanterns.

NOTES

NOTES

CHAPTER 6
IT'S ALL ABOUT GOALS

The following week Sherri continued to say her mantra out loud, she met with the coffeehouse crew twice, checked her groups in LinkedIn daily, and she wrote every day. For some reason she was feeling more energized at work. Reports flew off her desk in record time. She chatted with her co-workers during lunch. Her boss had even made a comment about how 'hyped up' and 'driven' Sherri was.

All in all it had been a very productive week. Even her writing seemed to improve.

Sherri felt like she was floating when she entered the warm cocoon of the coffee shop on Saturday.

Daniel was talking rapidly into his phone as she approached. He waved with a grin and pointed to the seat next to him. As she got settled, Sherri perused the table while her mentor finished up the call. There was a wide array of drawings, notes and doodles strewn over most of the tabletop. The scene contrasted sharply with the usually meticulously neat space Daniel kept.

With a relieved grunt Daniel set his phone down.

"Sorry about that. Trying to get things finished before this afternoon. Did you get some coffee?" he asked.

"Not yet. What's going on this afternoon?"

Daniel laughed, a hint of crazed hysteria creeping in. "What isn't going on? Nothing to worry about. Just a few self-imposed deadlines all hitting at the same time. When it rains it pours, right?"

Sherri cocked her head to the side trying to read Daniel's expression. He looked tired, but a good tired. Like someone who'd just finished a race or a final exam.

"How about you grab your latte and by the time you get back I'll have my mess cleaned up."

Sherri rose as a Daniel collected his papers and expertly paper clipped them into separate piles. By the time she'd returned Daniel looked his old serene self.

"How'd you do with your homework?"

Sherri hurriedly grabbed her computer case and extracted a brown folder. From it she took a small stack of typed paper and handed it to Daniel.

Reading quickly, he thumbed through her week's work, a look of deep concentration on his face. Sherri crossed her legs to keep them from shaking and took to tapping her thumbs together as she waited.

After what felt like eons to Sherri, Daniel looked up. Sherri winced as she took in his scowl.

"Did you really write this?" he asked.

Sherri nodded, nearly squeaking in response.

Slowly, a large grin spread across Daniel's countenance. "Not bad. Not bad at all."

Sherri beamed with pride. She knew it wasn't Shakespeare, but after reviewing her work, she'd recognized the depth of her writing. It was as if a part of her soul was finally coming out in a torrent of words.

"How did it feel?" Daniel asked.

"I…I've never felt so…full."

It was Daniel's turn to cock his head. "What do you mean?"

"I always knew something was missing. I just didn't know what. The feeling of getting my thoughts and feelings on paper just feels…fulfilling. I don't care if you and I are the only ones to read it. It still feels wonderful."

"I'm very happy for you, Sherri. You're starting to understand what the life of a writer entails. Now, are you ready for your next assignment?"

"Yes."

"Good." Daniel reached down and pulled a single sheet of paper out of his messenger bag. The paper was worn and ripped in more than one place. "I'm about to show you my master list, my dreams written as tangible goals. Wanna see?"

Sherri nodded wordlessly, anxious to get a private glimpse into Daniel's world. It only took her a moment to scan the page and look up.

"You're going to do all this aren't you?" she asked, admiration in her tone.

"I am. Has anyone ever told you that a dream is just a dream until you write it down?"

"I think so."

"Well, it's true. I never really believed it until I tried it for the first time."

"When was that?" Sherri asked.

"I wrote my first real goal when I decided to write my first book. It was on a sheet of lined paper I tore out from one of my old high school binders. I carried it around with me until my book was published. It simply said, 'I will publish a book.' Back then I didn't know how to do it right, but it worked. Now I know that goals have to be SMART."

"SMART?"

"Sorry. SMART is an acronym. It stands for Specific, Measurable, Achievable, Relevant and

Time-Bound. It's what every goal you write should have. In a nutshell, it means that every goal should meet certain requirements. I mentioned dreams. Dreams can be made into goals. But what if my dream was to be an Olympic gymnast? Is that really realistic? No. It's important to stretch your limits while being realistic.

"Let me break each part down and give you an example. The S stands for Specific. You need to write down exactly what you want to accomplish. This is the Who, What, Why part of your goal. Your goal is to write a book. So you want to specify what kind of book it is. It'll help you visualize the final product.

"The next part of SMART is Measurable. You need to measure whether you've accomplished your goal. With books it's pretty easy. You can say you want to write a fifty thousand word novel or a twenty chapter how-to book. Again, that's something that is measurable. It's like a mile marker that shows you how close you are to the finish line. Make sense so far?"

Sherri looked up from the notes she was taking. "Definitely. What about the rest of SMART?"

Daniel grinned enjoying Sherri's continued enthusiasm. "Achievable is next. Your goal has to have a realistic and achievable end state. To say, 'I'm going to write a one hundred thousand word novel in three days' isn't achievable."

Daniel paused to see if Sherri understood. She nodded.

"The next part, Relevant, is sort of a gut check. For writers, it's important to understand whether our stated goals take us where we want to go. For example, if I'm writing a science fiction series, and something inspires me to write a cozy mystery, does that make sense?"

Sherri shook her head.

Daniel continued. "I'm not saying we can't write in multiple genres, have multiple pen names or series. Keeping it relevant means having a larger vision for your goal. How does that book fit into the grand scheme of things? If you're working on a new brand and have thought through the building of the website, readership, etcetera, cool. It's just as important to be deliberate as it is to be creative.

"The last part of SMART goals is Time-Bound. That simply means you must have a deadline. I have a deadline for every one of my books. I know I have until January thirty first to finish a book. I also like to throw in intermediate goals along the way that act as stepping stones and gut checks to ensure I'm progressing at the rate I want."

"What happens if you don't meet your deadline?"

Daniel's face turned cold. "The secret writing police bust in, cuff you and send you to Alcatraz."

Sherri laughed as Daniel smirked.

"Kidding, of course. I'm very careful when I set my deadlines. You should be too. If you follow all the rules of SMART goals you won't miss. It really comes down to personal discipline. Remember, no one's putting a gun to your head. You have to keep on task and take your goals and deadlines seriously."

"What should my first goal be?" Sherri asked.

"That's your homework for this week!"

PRACTICE

Put your professional writer's cap on. Get it in your head that YOU are the boss and YOU are also the employee. Create a goal that is Specific, Measurable, Achievable, Relevant and Time-Bound.

Here are some examples:

- I will write 10,000 words every week for the sci-fi novel "Intergalactic Boggles".
- I will write a 20,000 word Amazon self-publishing tutorial for college students. The

first draft will be done by November 24th of this year.

- I will lose ten pounds by waking up every morning at 5:30am and going to the gym. I will also learn how to improve my diet from the book my friend Jimmy gave me. I will lose ten pounds by March 15th.

See how every goal listed is SMART in its own way? The more complicated the goal, the more complicated the stating of that goal.

NOTES

NOTES

CHAPTER 7

IN THE ZONE

Sherri was pretty organized and detail-oriented. Despite that fact, coming up with her first goal was tough. After multiple drafts, it was finally finished.

Meanwhile, she kept up with her daily writing and the every other day meetings at the coffee shop. The *'My name is…'* mantra came to her lips whenever she walked in front of a mirror. She could feel herself getting into a routine.

The following Saturday, Sherri stepped into the coffee shop with ease. Lacy, the barista, waved to her as she made her way to Daniel's table and slid her homework across the table.

Daniel caught it deftly and read the short paragraph. He looked up with a raised eyebrow.

"You sure you can handle this?" he asked.

A moment of indecision gripped Sherri's stomach. Willing it away by squaring her shoulders she said, "Yes I can."

Daniel smiled proudly. "I know you can."

While Sherri got comfortable, Daniel asked her how the week had gone. She told him.

"How do you think things are going?" he asked.

"Really well. What's next?"

"Let me ask you a question. Other than our last meeting when I had stuff scattered all over the place, have you ever seen my workspace look different?"

Sherri glanced at the table then back at Daniel. "I don't think so."

"Why do you think that is?"

Sherri shrugged. "Because you're obsessive compulsive?"

Daniel laughed. "Maybe a little. It's actually a little lesson I learned from one of my buddies that's big into Zen, Feng Shui and stuff. When I became a writer and actually started writing, I was always in a different place, using different writing materials, eating randomly. I found that I was never in my safe place, never in my zone."

Sherri frowned. "Why not?"

"When you start writing it's new and exciting. You're kinda flying by the seat of your pants. Pretty soon it's easy to lose focus. You combat that by coming up with a system and building your zone. When you do that the writing comes easier. What do you see when you look at my space?"

Sherri looked around Daniel and picked out what she thought was relevant. "You always have your computer and messenger bag. Oh, and the same notepad that you keep on the left side of the table."

Daniel smiled. "Good. Now let me tell you what you didn't notice." He patted his head. "I always wear a writing hat. I buy a new one for every book I write. This go-around it's a Detroit Tigers ball cap. I always listen to music with the same over-ear headphones. I make a soundtrack for each book I write. I always order the same green tea. I have the same cinnamon tea tree chewing sticks that I chew on while I'm writing. I know it sounds really strange, and yes maybe a bit obsessive compulsive, but all these things put me in my happy place. It's my writing zone."

"How do I find my happy place?"

"It might take you a little time, but pretty soon you'll make it a habit. Maybe you won't be able to write until you have the same fuzzy writing slippers on or pink scarf. I've got a friend that can't write without his yellow shooting glasses. Don't ask me what it does for his eyesight, but it works for him."

"So that's my homework?" Sherri asked.

"You got it. Experiment while you're writing this week. See what works and what doesn't. Come back next Saturday and give me a rundown."

PRACTICE

It's time to find your system, your zone, your happy place. What makes you feel comfortable when you're writing? Do you like to wear sweatpants and a tank top? Have you unconsciously brought the same snack for every writing session? How will you stay hydrated?

Write down what your writing props are and the places you feel most comfortable writing. Make sure these things add to your writing and are not a distraction.

NOTES

NOTES

CHAPTER 8
SUPPORTING CAST

Sherri completed her assignment quickly. Without knowing it, she'd already built her comfy writing zone. Her shiny computer was the tool, her latte served as caffeine sustenance, the banana nut muffin kept her just full enough and acted as a reward (she wouldn't take the first bite until she'd written one hundred words). It was easy to add locations (the coffee shop and the nook in her apartment that overlooked the park across the street) and other items like her old running shoes that felt more like slippers and the threadbare t-shirt she'd had since high school (she wore it under her sweater).

On Saturday, she handed the list to Daniel after placing her latte and muffin order with always smiling Lacy. Sherri waved to familiar faces as she waited for Daniel to finish.

"How's it feel?" Daniel asked while Sherri bit into her muffin.

"How does what feel?" Sherri asked through a mouthful of fluffy banana nut goodness.

"To be a writer."

Sherri chewed slowly and then swallowed, followed by a careful sip of her steaming latte.

"I...ummm, it feels good." There was a hint of the old Sherri in her tone.

"Are you sure? You don't sound like you believe it." Daniel's face was unreadable despite his customary smile.

Sherri fidgeted in her seat and put her coffee down.

She coughed the words quickly. "I guess I don't feel official yet. I know I say I'm a writer all day long, but I feel like something's missing."

Daniel just nodded and stared for a moment. "I want you to listen, Sherri. You are a writer. Since we've met, I've seen you take your writing career more seriously than most of the writers I've ever met. You need to understand that even though you might not have the fancy business cards or a high profile book tour, you are a writer."

Sherri sat up a little straighter at the stern lesson. She didn't want to disappoint Daniel. He'd done so much for her already.

"So why do I feel like I'm not...official?" Sherri asked, grasping at some newfound reserve of courage.

"I can't tell you when it will happen for you. For me, it wasn't until I press the publish button." A smile returned to Daniel's face, much to the relief of Sherri's frazzled nerves. "This week's homework might help you feel more official. How many words do you have written so far?"

Sherri perked up. The night before she'd asked herself the same question and looked down in surprise at the document word count on the computer.

"Just over ten thousand words," she answered.

"That's fantastic!" Daniel beamed. "Have you thought about a book cover?"

"I thought about it, but, well, I don't really have the money for it right now."

"How much do you think a book cover costs?"

Sherri tallied random numbers in her head then huffed. "I don't really know."

"I'll tell you this. Nowadays, a great book cover isn't nearly as expensive as you might think. This whole Internet thing means we can contract with talented designers all over the world. There are a lot of countries out there that have a lower cost of living than we do. You'll find that your money can go a lot farther with their talent. That brings me to this week's assignment. You need a supporting cast."

"A what?"

"A supporting cast. It's your team of experts working behind the scenes to make you look like a rock star."

The thought of having a team made Sherri's stomach turn. She wasn't exactly the leader type.

Daniel chuckled at the look on Sherri's face. "I know what you're thinking. You don't want the responsibility of running a team. That's not what I'm talking about. An author's supporting cast takes the place of the role a traditional publishing house might take. You'll need a designer, a proof reader, an editor, just to name three."

Sherri's face went paler. Daniel reached out and patted Sherri's hand. "Don't worry. It's not as bad as it sounds. Once you have some go-to contractors in place, you can really get rockin'." Daniel opened his bag and pulled out a single sheet of paper. "Here's my supporting cast. Talk to every one of them. I told them you'd be contacting them. Feel free to use all or none of them. You need to be comfortable with your team's abilities and personalities. These guys and gals all have websites. Take a look at their portfolios and testimonials."

Sherri stared at the neatly typed list of contacts and gulped hard.

"What if I can't do this?" she asked softly.

"First, I know you can. Second, if this isn't the route you want to go, there are agents and publishers out there that can take care of the grunt work for you, but they'll want a fee and possibly a portion of your royalties. I recommend you try to go it alone, with my help, of course. It'll give you a better feel for the industry, what works and what doesn't. It's kinda like buying a manufacturing company. You've gotta get in the factory to see how things are cranking or you'll be clueless."

Sherri wasn't so sure, but nodded. "Okay. I'll do it."

PRACTICE

You need to look for your supporting cast. Here's a list of experts you will need in your corner if you are serious about being a successful independent author. These are all contractors I have personally used and highly recommend.

- **Book Cover Designer:** You can either buy the rights to a pre-made cover or commission experts on a site like 99Designs.com. These two options are much more economical than hiring a single graphic designer.

- **Editor:** Proofreaders and editors come in all shapes and sizes. Find out whom other indie writers are using. Do an online search. Ask for pricing and dig into what they'll actually provide. Can't afford a pro? Print off ten copies of your manuscript and ask friends and colleagues to red pen it and give you honest feedback.

- **Book Formatting Specialist**: You will need different formatting for print books and ebooks. You can hire a company like 52Novels, use a contractor service like Elance.com, or learn to do it yourself.

- **Website designer**: You can either look for a company in your area, use Elance.com, or do it yourself on a platform like Wordpress and Weebly. You can also check out a new service that provides free blogs to authors at au-thor.com

--MASTER TIP--

Ask other authors. Use your Groups on LinkedIn to find out who other writers are using.

NOTES

NOTES

CHAPTER 9
A NEW PATH

It took Sherri two full days to muster the courage to contact any of the professionals Daniel had recommended. Once she had the first conversation with Daniel's book cover designer, she felt silly for ever feeling nervous. The designer answered all Sherri's questions and provided her with pricing and plenty of examples of his work.

The same happened with the editor, and on and on.

Not only that, she'd written another 5,000 words!

To say that she was on cloud nine would've been a major understatement in Sherri's mind. Walking into the coffee shop the following Saturday, Sherri felt like she was on top of the world.

As she stepped into the familiar confines, a cheer sounded from the back of the room. Sherri stopped dead in her tracks, a look of surprise stamped on her face.

At the opposite end of the shop, Daniel and her other new friends had crammed three tables together and they were all standing up, facing her, cheering. They were each holding up handwritten hot pink poster board signs. Sherri smiled meekly as she read them.

Congratulation Sherri!
Soon to be published super-writer Sherri.
Sherri Is a Writer
We Love Sherri

Tears welled up in her eyes as she scanned her friends.

"Now I hope those are happy tears, girl," boomed Frank and he walked over and gave her a big hug.

They each took turns giving her handshakes and embraces. After the commotion settled and the other patrons stopped staring, Sherri, Daniel and the coffeehouse crew took their seats.

"Do you like our little surprise?" asked Patrice.

"Thank you all so much. I…I don't know what to say," answered Sherri, still shocked by the reception.

"Say you'll get us all copies of your book!" laughed Frank.

"Of course! I owe you all so much."

Daniel rapped his knuckles on table.

"I'd like to offer a toast to our new friend Sherri. Her new book will be finished in two months and we couldn't be more proud of her. Welcome to the family, Sherri!"

Everyone clinked their coffee mugs together. Sherri soaked up the feeling and filed it away as one of the happiest moments of her life. She'd finally found real meaning. She'd found people who liked and respected her. She'd found a craft that she loved.

Sherri raised her hand and the group quieted again.

"Now that I know I'm a writer, I write every day, I've got my goals, I've set my deadlines, I'm building my team…how do I get published?" Sherri asked.

The rest of the coffeehouse crew smiled and turned their collective gaze to Daniel.

In a passable southern drawl, Daniel said, "That, my dear, is a story for another day."

* * * * *

I hope you've enjoyed this story. If you did, please leave a review on Amazon. Reviews are, after all, the lifeblood of any author ☺

If you'd like to know more about writing and self-publishing, please visit me at CarlosCooper.com.

Oh, and don't forget to claim your FREE author blog at au-thor.com.

Now get back to writing!

* * * * *

NOTES

NOTES

RESOURCES MENTIONED IN THE BOOK

au-thor.com: Free author blogs and additional resources for authors

Elance.com: Online contractor source for many services.

99Designs.com: Graphic designers compete to design you the best book cover or logo. You pick the winner.

LinkedIn.com: Professional social network. Great for building your resume, building a network and sharing ideas with peers.

TheWritePractice.com: Get daily writing practice and mingle with other writers.

Made in the USA
Charleston, SC
15 December 2013